wedding shit

plan shit

WEDDING DATE :

VENUE:

BUDGET:

OFFICIANT:

WEDDING PARTY:

NOTES & REMINDERS:

budget shit

	TOTAL COST:	DEPOSIT:	REMAINDER:
WEDDING VENUE			
RECEPTION VENUE			
FLORIST			
OFFICIANT			
CATERER			
WEDDING CAKE			
BRIDAL ATTIRE			
GROOM ATTIRE			
BRIDAL JEWELRY			
BRIDESMAID ATTIRE			
GROOMSMEN ATTIRE			
HAIR & MAKE UP			
PHOTOGRAPHER			
VIDEOGRAPHER			
DJ SERVICE/ENTERTAINMENT			
INVITATIONS			
TRANSPORTATION			
WEDDING PARTY GIFTS			
RENTALS			
HONEYMOON			

budget shit

	TOTAL COST:	DEPOSIT:	REMAINDER:

budget shit

	TOTAL COST:	DEPOSIT:	REMAINDER:

12 months before

- ~~SET THE DATE~~
- SET YOUR BUDGET
- CHOOSE YOUR THEME
- ORGANIZE ENGAGEMENT PARTY
- ~~RESEARCH VENUES~~
- BOOK A WEDDING PLANNER
- RESEARCH PHOTOGRAPHERS
- RESEARCH VIDEOGRAPHERS
- RESEARCH DJ'S/ENTERTAINMENT

- CONSIDER FLORISTS
- RESEARCH CATERERS
- DECIDE ON OFFICIANT
- ~~CREATE INITIAL GUEST LIST~~
- CHOOSE WEDDING PARTY
- SHOP FOR WEDDING DRESS
- REGISTER WITH GIFT REGISTRY
- DISCUSS HONEYMOON IDEAS
- RESEARCH WEDDING RINGS

THINGS TO REMEMBER:

checklist

FOR : DATE ✓

9 months before

- FINALIZE GUEST LIST
- ORDER INVITATIONS
- PLAN YOUR RECEPTION
- BOOK PHOTOGRAPHER
- BOOK VIDEOGRAPHER
- BOOK FLORIST
- BOOK DJ/ENTERTAINMENT
- BOOK CATERER
- CHOOSE WEDDING CAKE

- CHOOSE WEDDING GOWN
- ORDER BRIDESMAIDS DRESSES
- RESERVE TUXEDOS
- ARRANGE TRANSPORTATION
- BOOK WEDDING VENUE
- BOOK RECEPTION VENUE
- PLAN HONEYMOON
- BOOK OFFICIANT
- BOOK ROOMS FOR GUESTS

THINGS TO REMEMBER:

checklist

FOR : DATE ✓

6 months before

- ORDER THANK YOU NOTES
- REVIEW RECEPTION DETAILS
- MAKE APPT FOR DRESS FITTING
- CONFIRM BRIDEMAIDS DRESSES
- GET MARRIAGE LICENSE

- BOOK HAIR/MAKE UP STYLIST
- CONFIRM MUSIC SELECTIONS
- PLAN BRIDAL SHOWER
- PLAN REHEARSAL
- SHOP FOR WEDDING RINGS

THINGS TO REMEMBER:

checklist

FOR : DATE ✓

3 months before

- MAIL OUT INVITATIONS
- MEET WITH OFFICIANT
- BUY GIFTS FOR WEDDING PARTY
- BOOK FINAL GOWN FITTING
- BUY WEDDING BANDS
- PLAN YOUR HAIR STYLE
- PURCHASE SHOES/HEELS
- CONFIRM PASSPORTS ARE VALID

- FINALIZE RECEPTION MENU
- PLAN REHEARSAL DINNER
- CONFIRM ALL BOOKINGS
- APPLY FOR MARRIAGE LICENSE
- CONFIRM MUSIC SELECTIONS
- DRAFT WEDDING VOWS
- CHOOSE YOUR MC
- ARRANGE AIRPORT TRANSFER

THINGS TO REMEMBER:

checklist

FOR :   DATE   ✓

1 month before

- CONFIRM FINAL GUEST COUNT
- CONFIRM RECEPTION DETAILS
- ATTEND FINAL GOWN FITTING
- CONFIRM PHOTOGRAPHER
- WRAP WEDDING PARTY GIFTS
- CREATE PHOTOGRAPHY SHOT LIST

- REHEARSE WEDDING VOWS
- BOOK MANI-PEDI
- CONFIRM WITH FLORIST
- CONFIRM VIDEOGRAPHER
- PICK UP BRIDEMAIDS DRESSES
- CREATE WEDDING SCHEDULE

THINGS TO REMEMBER:

checklist

FOR : DATE ✓

1 week before

FINALIZE SEATING PLANS

MAKE PAYMENTS TO VENDORS

PACK FOR HONEYMOON

CONFIRM HOTEL RESERVATIONS

DELIVER LICENSE TO OFFICIANT

CONFIRM WITH BAKERY

PICK UP WEDDING DRESS

PICK UP TUXEDOS

THINGS TO REMEMBER:

checklist

FOR : DATE ✓

1 day before

GET MANICURE/PEDICURE

GIVE GIFTS TO WEDDING PARTY

ATTEND REHEARSAL DINNER

FINALIZE PACKING

GET A GOOD NIGHT'S SLEEP!

TO DO LIST:

checklist

FOR :   DATE   ✓

the big day

HEALTHY BREAKFAST

GET HAIR & MAKE UP DONE

ENJOY YOUR BIG DAY!

GIVE RINGS TO BEST MAN

MEET WITH BRIDESMAIDS

TO DO LIST:

checklist

FOR :   DATE   ✓

party shit

ENGAGEMENT PARTY:

DATE: LOCATION:

TIME: NUMBER OF GUESTS:

NOTES:

BRIDAL SHOWER:

DATE: LOCATION:

TIME: NUMBER OF GUESTS:

NOTES:

STAG & DOE PARTY:

DATE: LOCATION:

TIME: NUMBER OF GUESTS:

NOTES:

checklist

FOR :   DATE   ✓

wedding party

MAID/MATRON OF HONOR:

PHONE:　　　　　　　　DRESS SIZE:　　　　　　　　SHOE SIZE:

EMAIL:

BRIDESMAID:

PHONE:　　　　　　　　DRESS SIZE:　　　　　　　　SHOE SIZE:

EMAIL:

BRIDESMAID #2:

PHONE:　　　　　　　　DRESS SIZE:　　　　　　　　SHOE SIZE:

EMAIL:

BRIDESMAID #3:

PHONE:　　　　　　　　DRESS SIZE:　　　　　　　　SHOE SIZE:

EMAIL:

BRIDESMAID #4:

PHONE:　　　　　　　　DRESS SIZE:　　　　　　　　SHOE SIZE:

EMAIL:

NOTES:

checklist

FOR :   DATE   ✓

wedding party

BEST MAN:

PHONE: WAIST SIZE: SHOE SIZE:

NECK SIZE: SLEEVE SIZE: JACKET SIZE:

EMAIL:

GROOMSMEN #1:

PHONE: WAIST SIZE: SHOE SIZE:

NECK SIZE: SLEEVE SIZE: JACKET SIZE:

EMAIL:

GROOMSMEN #2:

PHONE: WAIST SIZE: SHOE SIZE:

NECK SIZE: SLEEVE SIZE: JACKET SIZE:

EMAIL:

GROOMSMEN #3:

PHONE: WAIST SIZE: SHOE SIZE:

NECK SIZE: SLEEVE SIZE: JACKET SIZE:

EMAIL:

GROOMSMEN #4:

PHONE: WAIST SIZE: SHOE SIZE:

NECK SIZE: SLEEVE SIZE: JACKET SIZE:

EMAIL:

checklist

FOR : DATE ✓

photographer

PHOTOGRAPHER:

PHONE: COMPANY:

EMAIL: ADDRESS:

WEDDING PACKAGE OVERVIEW:

EST PRICE:

INCLUSIONS: YES ✓   NO ✓   COST:

ENGAGEMENT SHOOT:

PHOTO ALBUMNS:

FRAMES:

PROOFS INCLUDED:

NEGATIVES INCLUDED:

TOTAL COST:

NOTES:

checklist

FOR :   DATE   ✓

videographer

VIDEOGRAPHER:

PHONE: COMPANY:

EMAIL: ADDRESS:

WEDDING PACKAGE OVERVIEW:

EST PRICE:

INCLUSIONS: YES ✓ NO ✓ COST:

DUPLICATES/COPIES:

PHOTO MONTAGE:

MUSIC ADDED:

EDITING:

TOTAL COST:

NOTES:

checklist

FOR : DATE ✓

DJ/entertainment

DJ/LIVE BAND/ENTERTAINMENT:

PHONE: COMPANY:

EMAIL: ADDRESS:

START TIME: END TIME:

ENTERTAINMENT SERVICE OVERVIEW:

EST PRICE:

INCLUSIONS: YES ✓ NO ✓ COST:

SOUND EQUIPMENT:

LIGHTING:

SPECIAL EFFECTS:

GRATUITIES

TOTAL COST:

NOTES:

checklist

FOR : DATE ✓

florist

FLORIST:

PHONE: COMPANY:

EMAIL: ADDRESS:

FLORAL PACKAGE:

EST PRICE: _____

INCLUSIONS: YES ✓ NO ✓ COST:

BRIDAL BOUQUET:

THROW AWAY BOUQUET:

CORSAGES:

CEREMONY FLOWERS

CENTERPIECES

CAKE TOPPER

BOUTONNIERE

TOTAL COST:

checklist

FOR : DATE ✓

wedding cake

PHONE: COMPANY:

EMAIL: ADDRESS:

WEDDING CAKE PACKAGE:

COST: _____ FREE TASTING: _____ DELIVERY FEE: _____

FLAVOR:

FILLING:

SIZE:

SHAPE:

COLOR:

EXTRAS:

TOTAL COST:

NOTES:

checklist

FOR :   DATE   ✓

transportation shit

TO CEREMONY: PICK UP TIME: PICK UP LOCATION:

BRIDE:

GROOM:

BRIDE'S PARENTS:

GROOM'S PARENTS:

BRIDESMAIDS:

GROOMSMEN:

NOTES:

TO RECEPTION: PICK UP TIME: PICK UP LOCATION:

BRIDE & GROOM:

BRIDE'S PARENTS:

GROOM'S PARENTS:

BRIDESMAIDS:

GROOMSMEN:

more party shit

BACHELORETTE PARTY:

DATE:

LOCATION:

TIME:

NUMBER OF GUESTS:

NOTES:

BACHELOR PARTY:

DATE:

LOCATION:

TIME:

NUMBER OF GUESTS:

NOTES:

CEREMONY REHEARSAL:

DATE:

LOCATION:

TIME:

NUMBER OF GUESTS:

NOTES:

reception shit

REHEARSAL DINNER:

DATE: LOCATION:

TIME: NUMBER OF GUESTS:

NOTES:

RECEPTION:

DATE: LOCATION:

TIME: NUMBER OF GUESTS:

NOTES:

REMINDERS:

break that shit down

GOAL   STEPS TO MAKE IT HAPPEN   DEADLINE   ✓

GOAL   STEPS TO MAKE IT HAPPEN   DEADLINE   ✓

GOAL   STEPS TO MAKE IT HAPPEN   DEADLINE   ✓

break that shit down

| GOAL | STEPS TO MAKE IT HAPPEN | DEADLINE | ✓ |

| GOAL | STEPS TO MAKE IT HAPPEN | DEADLINE | ✓ |

| GOAL | STEPS TO MAKE IT HAPPEN | DEADLINE | ✓ |

break that shit down

GOAL   STEPS TO MAKE IT HAPPEN   DEADLINE   ✓

GOAL   STEPS TO MAKE IT HAPPEN   DEADLINE   ✓

GOAL   STEPS TO MAKE IT HAPPEN   DEADLINE   ✓

break that shit down

GOAL	STEPS TO MAKE IT HAPPEN	DEADLINE	✓

GOAL	STEPS TO MAKE IT HAPPEN	DEADLINE	✓

GOAL	STEPS TO MAKE IT HAPPEN	DEADLINE	✓

break that shit down

GOAL   STEPS TO MAKE IT HAPPEN   DEADLINE   ✓

GOAL   STEPS TO MAKE IT HAPPEN   DEADLINE   ✓

GOAL   STEPS TO MAKE IT HAPPEN   DEADLINE   ✓

break that shit down

| GOAL | STEPS TO MAKE IT HAPPEN | DEADLINE | ✓ |

| GOAL | STEPS TO MAKE IT HAPPEN | DEADLINE | ✓ |

| GOAL | STEPS TO MAKE IT HAPPEN | DEADLINE | ✓ |

break that shit down

GOAL STEPS TO MAKE IT HAPPEN DEADLINE ✓

GOAL STEPS TO MAKE IT HAPPEN DEADLINE ✓

GOAL STEPS TO MAKE IT HAPPEN DEADLINE ✓

break that shit down

GOAL	STEPS TO MAKE IT HAPPEN	DEADLINE	✓

GOAL	STEPS TO MAKE IT HAPPEN	DEADLINE	✓

GOAL	STEPS TO MAKE IT HAPPEN	DEADLINE	✓

break that shit down

GOAL　　　　　　　STEPS TO MAKE IT HAPPEN　　　　DEADLINE　✓

GOAL　　　　　　　STEPS TO MAKE IT HAPPEN　　　　DEADLINE　✓

GOAL　　　　　　　STEPS TO MAKE IT HAPPEN　　　　DEADLINE　✓

break that shit down

| GOAL | STEPS TO MAKE IT HAPPEN | DEADLINE | ✓ |

| GOAL | STEPS TO MAKE IT HAPPEN | DEADLINE | ✓ |

| GOAL | STEPS TO MAKE IT HAPPEN | DEADLINE | ✓ |

break that shit down

| GOAL | STEPS TO MAKE IT HAPPEN | DEADLINE | ✓ |

| GOAL | STEPS TO MAKE IT HAPPEN | DEADLINE | ✓ |

| GOAL | STEPS TO MAKE IT HAPPEN | DEADLINE | ✓ |

break that shit down

GOAL	STEPS TO MAKE IT HAPPEN	DEADLINE	✓

GOAL	STEPS TO MAKE IT HAPPEN	DEADLINE	✓

GOAL	STEPS TO MAKE IT HAPPEN	DEADLINE	✓

break that shit down

GOAL   STEPS TO MAKE IT HAPPEN   DEADLINE   ✓

GOAL   STEPS TO MAKE IT HAPPEN   DEADLINE   ✓

GOAL   STEPS TO MAKE IT HAPPEN   DEADLINE   ✓

names & addresses

CEREMONY:

PHONE: CONTACT NAME:

EMAIL: ADDRESS:

RECEPTION:

PHONE: CONTACT NAME:

EMAIL: ADDRESS:

OFFICIANT:

PHONE: CONTACT NAME:

EMAIL: ADDRESS:

WEDDING PLANNER:

PHONE: CONTACT NAME:

EMAIL: ADDRESS:

CATERER:

PHONE: CONTACT NAME:

EMAIL: ADDRESS:

FLORIST:

PHONE: CONTACT NAME:

EMAIL: ADDRESS:

names & addresses

BAKERY:

PHONE: CONTACT NAME:

EMAIL: ADDRESS:

BRIDAL SHOP:

PHONE: CONTACT NAME:

EMAIL: ADDRESS:

PHOTOGRAPHER:

PHONE: CONTACT NAME:

EMAIL: ADDRESS:

VIDEOGRAPHER:

PHONE: CONTACT NAME:

EMAIL: ADDRESS:

DJ/ENTERTAINMENT:

PHONE: CONTACT NAME:

EMAIL: ADDRESS:

HAIR/NAIL SALON:

PHONE: CONTACT NAME:

EMAIL: ADDRESS:

names & addresses

RENTALS:

PHONE: CONTACT NAME:

EMAIL: ADDRESS:

HONEYMOON RESORT/HOTEL:

PHONE: CONTACT NAME:

EMAIL: ADDRESS:

TRANSPORTATION SERVICE:

PHONE: CONTACT NAME:

EMAIL: ADDRESS:

NOTES

caterer details

CONTACT INFORMATION:

PHONE:

CONTACT NAME:

EMAIL:

ADDRESS:

MENU CHOICE #1:

MENU CHOICE #2:

MENU CHOICE #3:

YES ✓ NO ✓ COST:

BAR INCLUDED:

CORKAGE FEE:

HORS D'OEURS:

TAXES INCLUDED:

GRATUITIES INCLUDED:

menu planner

HORS D'OEUVRES

1st COURSE:

2nd COURSE:

3rd COURSE:

4th COURSE:

DESSERTS:

menu planner

COFFEE/TEA:

FRUIT:

SWEETS TABLE:

WEDDING CAKE:

NOTES:

more shit...

DATE:

DATE:

DATE:

DATE:

DATE:

DATE:

more shit...

DATE:

DATE:

DATE:

DATE:

DATE:

DATE:

more shit...

DATE:

DATE:

DATE:

DATE:

DATE:

DATE:

more shit...

DATE:

DATE:

DATE:

DATE:

DATE:

DATE:

more shit...

DATE:

DATE:

DATE:

DATE:

DATE:

DATE:

more shit...

DATE:

DATE:

DATE:

DATE:

DATE:

DATE:

more shit...

DATE:

DATE:

DATE:

DATE:

DATE:

DATE:

more shit...

DATE:

DATE:

DATE:

DATE:

DATE:

DATE:

more shit...

DATE:

DATE:

DATE:

DATE:

DATE:

DATE:

more shit...

DATE:

DATE:

DATE:

DATE:

DATE:

DATE:

more shit...

DATE:

DATE:

DATE:

DATE:

DATE:

DATE:

more shit...

DATE:

DATE:

DATE:

DATE:

DATE:

DATE:

more shit...

DATE:

DATE:

DATE:

DATE:

DATE:

DATE:

1 week before

THINGS TO DO: NOTES:

MONDAY

TUESDAY

WEDNESDAY

THURSDAY

REMINDERS & NOTES:

1 week before

THINGS TO DO: NOTES:

FRIDAY

SATURDAY

SUNDAY

LEFT TO DO:

REMINDERS: NOTES:

guest list

NAME:	ADDRESS:	# IN PARTY:	RSVP: ✓

guest list

NAME:	ADDRESS:	# IN PARTY:	RSVP: ✓

guest list

NAME:	ADDRESS:	# IN PARTY:	RSVP: ✓

guest list

NAME:	ADDRESS:	# IN PARTY:	RSVP: ✓

guest list

NAME:	ADDRESS:	# IN PARTY:	RSVP: ✓

guest list

NAME:	ADDRESS:	# IN PARTY:	RSVP: ✓

guest list

NAME:	ADDRESS:	# IN PARTY:	RSVP: ✓

guest list

NAME:	ADDRESS:	# IN PARTY:	RSVP: ✓

guest list

NAME:	ADDRESS:	# IN PARTY:	RSVP: ✓

guest list

NAME:	ADDRESS:	# IN PARTY:	RSVP: ✓

guest list

NAME:	ADDRESS:	# IN PARTY:	RSVP: ✓

guest list

NAME:	ADDRESS:	# IN PARTY:	RSVP: ✓

guest list

NAME:	ADDRESS:	# IN PARTY:	RSVP: ✓

guest list

NAME:	ADDRESS:	# IN PARTY:	RSVP: ✓

guest list

NAME:	ADDRESS:	# IN PARTY:	RSVP: ✓

guest list

NAME:	ADDRESS:	# IN PARTY:	RSVP: ✓

guest list

NAME:	ADDRESS:	# IN PARTY:	RSVP: ✓

guest list

NAME:	ADDRESS:	# IN PARTY:	RSVP: ✓

guest list

NAME:	ADDRESS:	# IN PARTY:	RSVP: ✓

guest list

NAME:	ADDRESS:	# IN PARTY:	RSVP: ✓

guest list

NAME:	ADDRESS:	# IN PARTY:	RSVP: ✓

guest list

NAME:	ADDRESS:	# IN PARTY:	RSVP: ✓

guest list

NAME:	ADDRESS:	# IN PARTY:	RSVP: ✓

guest list

NAME:	ADDRESS:	# IN PARTY:	RSVP: ✓

guest list

NAME:	ADDRESS:	# IN PARTY:	RSVP: ✓

guest list

NAME:	ADDRESS:	# IN PARTY:	RSVP: ✓

guest list

NAME:	ADDRESS:	# IN PARTY:	RSVP: ✓

guest list

NAME:	ADDRESS:	# IN PARTY:	RSVP: ✓

guest list

NAME:	ADDRESS:	# IN PARTY:	RSVP: ✓

guest list

NAME:	ADDRESS:	# IN PARTY:	RSVP: ✓

guest list

NAME:	ADDRESS:	# IN PARTY:	RSVP: ✓

guest list

NAME:	ADDRESS:	# IN PARTY:	RSVP: ✓

guest list

NAME:	ADDRESS:	# IN PARTY:	RSVP: ✓

guest list

NAME:	ADDRESS:	# IN PARTY:	RSVP: ✓

guest list

NAME:	ADDRESS:	# IN PARTY:	RSVP: ✓

guest list

NAME:	ADDRESS:	# IN PARTY:	RSVP: ✓

guest list

NAME:	ADDRESS:	# IN PARTY:	RSVP: ✓

guest list

NAME:	ADDRESS:	# IN PARTY:	RSVP: ✓

guest list

NAME:	ADDRESS:	# IN PARTY:	RSVP: ✓

guest list

NAME:	ADDRESS:	# IN PARTY:	RSVP: ✓

guest list

NAME:	ADDRESS:	# IN PARTY:	RSVP: ✓

guest list

NAME:	ADDRESS:	# IN PARTY:	RSVP: ✓

guest list

NAME:	ADDRESS:	# IN PARTY:	RSVP: ✓

guest list

NAME:	ADDRESS:	# IN PARTY:	RSVP: ✓

guest list

NAME:	ADDRESS:	# IN PARTY:	RSVP: ✓

guest list

NAME:	ADDRESS:	# IN PARTY:	RSVP: ✓

guest list

NAME:	ADDRESS:	# IN PARTY:	RSVP: ✓

guest list

NAME:	ADDRESS:	# IN PARTY:	RSVP: ✓

guest list

NAME:	ADDRESS:	# IN PARTY:	RSVP: ✓

seating planner

Table#

Table#

seating planner

Table#

Table#

seating planner

Table#

Table#

seating planner

Table#

Table#

seating planner

Table#

Table#

seating planner

Table#

Table#

seating planner

Table#

Table#

seating planner

Table#

Table#

seating planner

Table#

Table#

seating planner

Table#

Table#

seating planner

Table#

Table#

seating planner

Table#

Table#

seating planner

Table#

Table#

seating planner

Table#

Table#

seating planner

Table#

Table#

seating planner

Table#

Table#

seating planner

Table#

Table#

seating planner

Table#

Table#

seating planner

Table#

Table#

seating planner

Table#

Table#

seating planner

Table#

Table#

seating planner

Table#

Table#

seating planner

Table#

Table#

seating planner

Table#

Table#

seating planner

Table#

Table#

seating planner

Table#

Table#

seating planner

Table#

Table#

Made in the USA
Middletown, DE
18 May 2019